New Canadian Poetry

Fitzhenry & Whiteside Limited
195 Allstate Parkway
Markham, Ontario L3R 4T8

In the United States:
121 Harvard Avenue, Suite 2
Allston, Massachusetts 02134

www.fitzhenry.ca
godwit@fitzhenry.ca

Canadian Cataloguing in Publication Data
Main entry under title:
New Canadian poetry
ISBN 1-55041-606-5
1. Canadian poetry (English) — 20th century. I. Jones, Evan, 1973- .

PS8293.N478 2000   C811'.5408   C00-930247-6
PR9195.7.N388 2000

Design by Karen Petherick

Cover Detail: Anthony (Tony) Morse URQUHART,
Niagara Falls with a Collection of Famous Daredevils, 1968
Government of Ontario Art Collection, photographed by
Thomas Moore Photography, Toronto
CARfac©Collective

Printed and bound in Canada

New Canadian Poe

Edited by Evan Jones

Introduction by A.F. Moritz

Fitzhenry & Whiteside

Contents

Acknowledgements

Brian Bartlett's "Always" reprinted with permission from *Granite Erratics* (Victoria: Ekstasis Editions, 1997). "The Afterlife of Trees" originally appeared in *Event*.

Lucy Brennan's "Sweeney and the Scholars" and "Betwixt and Between" reprinted with permission from *Migrants All* (Toronto: watershedBooks, 1999).

Anne Compton's "The Mermaid's Singing" and "Lightwork in Vermeer" appeared previously in *The Malahat Review*. "Unreadable Flowers" appeared in *Descant*.

Mary Dalton's "Burn" appeared previously in *The Fiddlehead*. "The Tall World of Their Torn Stories" appeared in *TickleAce*. It won the inaugural TickleAce Cabot Award for poetry in 1998.

Lynn Davies' "The Cherry Tree," "Cape Enrage" and "Hartlen Point" reprinted with permission from *The Bridge That Carries The Road* (London: Brick Books, 1999).

Iain Deans' "Insects" appeared previously in *The New Quarterly*.

Jeffery Donaldson's "Feddy Doe" reprinted with permission from *Waterglass* (Montreal: McGill-Queen's, 1999).

John Donlan's "Mirage" reprinted with permission from *Domestic Economy* (London: Brick Books, 1990, reprinted 1997). "Tilt" and "Picture" reprinted with permission from *Green Man* (Vancouver: Ronsdale Press, 1999).

jodi essery's "still life with pomegranate" appeared previously in *ultra-violet*.

Albert Fuller's "children who hunger for space" reprinted with permission from *flowers in the empty house* (Toronto: watershedBooks, 1998).

Carla Hartsfield's "Playing" reprinted with permission from *The Invisible Moon* (Montreal: Signal Editions/Véhicule Press, 1988).

Ricardo Sternberg's "Map of Dreams (I, Diogo, son of Juan)" reprinted with permission from *Map of Dreams* (Montreal: Signal Editions/Véhicule Press, 1996). "Jonah" appeared previously in *Descant*.

John Terpstra's "To God, as a Small Pest" reprinted with permission from *Devil's Punch Bowl* (Toronto: The St. Thomas Poetry Series, 1998). "James Joyce and the Equator" reprinted with permission from *Forty Days and Forty Nights* (Windsor: Netherlandic Press, 1987).

Priscila Uppal's "How to Draw Blood From a Stone" and "Bone-marrow" reprinted with permission from *How to Draw Blood From a Stone* (Toronto: Exile Editions, 1998).

Linda Waybrant's "the colour of flight" reprinted from *The Colour of Flight*, with permission from the author and Wolsak & Wynn Publishers Ltd, Toronto, Canada.

Introduction

Poetry, the only high art besides painting that has been practised
continuously in Canada since Confederation, continues to work out
answers to the Canadian question: What unique character can be
forged for an offshoot nation, which uses a language shared with older
and more powerful relatives, and at the same time possesses an
unprecedented mixture of human ingredients and conditions? This is
serious, but it is also a matter of adventure and play, which are neces-
sary for growth and discovery: "We praise constancy as brave,/But
variation's lovelier," says John Newlove. *New Canadian Poetry*, an
exemplary sampler of our current poetry, displays both its earnestness
and its excitement in choice poems by some of the best emerging
poets.

The poets collected by Evan Jones build upon and interrogate
their predecessors' work, fulfilling Al Purdy's prophecy of the
successors that will come:

> They are so different these small ones
> their green hair shines
> they lift their bodies high in light
> they droop in rain and move in unison
> toward some lost remembered place
> we came from like a question...

These poets make new contributions to the constant discovery, or
invention, of the Canadian difference, but not in any crudely explicit
manner. They rely not on proclamations but on a fact about poetry:
the most dynamic shaping of language, which is our most deeply and
characteristically human element, good poetry inevitably takes into
itself the whole fact of a people's character through the people's
speech.

To a reader of *New Canadian Poetry*, it may seem a distant era in
which Margaret Atwood's Susanna Moodie wondered, "is it my own
lack/of conviction which makes/these vistas of desolation", and self-

critically concluded, "I am a word/in a foreign language". However, the task of remaking foreign words into the Canadian language always remains, and these new poets are working at it. One element to listen for in them is an intensified language developed through a new sense of freedom to choose and mix:

> And I was Orpheus the wrong way round
> climbing from the dream spaces of a life...

and,

> ...letting eternity flow over a sill
> in parody of earthlight...

and,

> They keep for themselves only one or two truths—
> some early Eden, a clean weapon...

What is accepted is the liberty to adapt from all sources every sort of formal, lyrical, philosophical, and rhetorical idea.

But is this not merely a redoubling of the globalism that characterizes modernity? The form it takes now in Canada is a response to shortcomings that poets have felt in their poetic tradition and the national culture. There has been, they think, too much nature meditation in free verse of a lax, standardized sort. And too much of a simplistic, often documentary or editorializing approach to Canada itself.

There is no mere nationalism here. This Canadianism is not only a building up of the nation's voice but a breaking down of that voice, a needed destruction of whatever has been merely nostalgic or ideological. These poets insist simply on discovering and creating themselves, their place, and their time, in the most intense terms possible, using the richest and most diverse materials they can come by. How better to manifest and help create their nation? For it is poetry and the common life of the people which actually enact what politicians know only as cliche: that the nation is the free creativity of its every member. Always these new poets are seeking a language that gives our creative life its full complexity and stays in close contact with its origins. As one of them says, in words that could describe the poetic voice:

> she whirs it out a bird's way, into the narrowest island's wind,
> to where the coughings of crows go—resolved to be caught
> solely by the tuned ears of fishermen...

Given its insistence upon originality and artistic distinction, we should expect our current poetry to be diverse. The poets included here come from across the country. They are not from one "generation": their birth dates range from 1931 to 1976. Their styles and subject matter are varied, too. What links them is their way of combining experimentation with excellence and finish. They possess both adventure and elegance. From recent books and magazines Mr. Jones has well chosen poets who, whatever their age, are participating in an intensified concern for a powerful yet sophisticated utterance.

And so, what these poets chiefly share is a renewed commitment to the ancient art of poetry, its incomparable fund of possibilities and its traditional gift of creative, emotional, and intellectual dynamism to whoever can practice it truly. On every page of *New Canadian Poetry* the alert reader will find faithfulness to the joyous impulse and the needed labour of embodying self, home, and native place, of criticizing them and prophesying change, and of making something new out of ourselves, through our language. As one of these poets writes about those who "go looking for promises":

> these are the children who believe in what lives
> beyond the end of the corridor
> that there is sunlight waiting to enter their eyes
> a spaciousness wanting their touch
> a secret to be unfolded like a vast landscape

A.F. Moritz, Toronto, January 2000

Brian Bartlett

Brian Bartlett (1953-) was born in St. Stephen, New Brunswick, and now lives in Halifax, Nova Scotia. He has published several collections of poems, most recently *Granite Erratics* and *Underwater Carpentry*. A recipient of two *Malahat Review* long poem prizes, he also publishes fiction and other kinds of prose.

The Afterlife of Trees
(for Don McKay)

Neither sheep nor cows criss-cross our lives as much.
Trees dangle apples and nuts for the hungry, throw
shade down for lovers, mark sites for the lost,
and first and last are
utterly themselves,
fuller and finer than any number or letter,
any 7 or T. Their fragmentary afterlife goes on
in a guitar's body and a hockey stick, in the beaked faces
up a totem pole and the stake through a vampire's heart,
in a fragrant cheese-board, a Welsh love-spoon,
a giant green dragonfly suspended from the ceiling
with twine, the handle of an axe that splits kindling
all winter, in the spellbinding shapechanging
behind a glass woodstove-door...

and in a table I sanded and finished this week.
—*Finished?*—Four grades of sandpaper drew out
alder's "nature," inimitable amoeba shapes,
waves, half-moons, paw prints dissolving in mud.
What looks more beautiful after death? We sand
and sand, but under the stain, beyond out pottery
and books, our fallen hairs trapped in the varnish,
something remains like memories of a buck
rubbing its horns on bark. Soaked in
deeper than even the grain goes: cries, whistles, hoots.

A Toss of Cones

Twelve months, and one more ring to the tree—
a measurement of years, hidden as our marrow.
Show me a table that grows like that.

No alder chair lets leaves go in October
and unfolds others in May. No birch garden-stake
twists to left or right, hungry for sunlight.
A bird's-eye-maple bowl doesn't throw
many-branched shadows over the ground
any more than ashes broadcast on the wind
are a man or woman remembered and mourned.

Don't talk to me about the afterlife of trees.
I need places where sap drops in a bucket
and jack pines start up through fire-blackened soil,

where wingseeds spin down through air, a toss
of cones on the orange earth.

In this world in a minute you can walk—for now,
you can walk—from dim woods where firs squeeze
out other firs, like too many fish feeding in a pool,

to one butternut tree on a river bank
spreading its limbs like an embrace of the air.

After breathing paper too long, be glad to know
a white elm drinks fifteen hundred gallons of water
from a hot dawn to a hot dusk

and Moroccan goats climb to the highest branches
                                    of argan trees
to eat the sweet leaves and bark.

Always

Somewhere a wolf spider dances on a white rock
shaking in fervent frenzy. Somewhere a crippled auk
tries to fly, kildeer mate in a soccer field, a shrike
shoves a warbler onto a thorn. At this moment
a woman watches a meteor, a child counts the seconds
between lightning and thunder, old men share
ale made from malt, hops, and Scottish water.
Always, during your day and during your night
black flies pierce human skin, rice-shoots
poke through earth, worms tunnel, a mother grazes
her infant's cheek with love for the first time.
Always, heat at the heart of a crematorium is reaching
its peak, and a queen bee drops dead into mud. Pick
any moment: a couple on a mountain breathe air too thin
for their lungs, but feel inexplicably at home,
while a couple wandering in their garden
smell the blossoms of two dozen species, and feel lifted
into an exotic place. Now, as I write, rain cascades
into a shrunken stream, foxes nip each other,
a rotting peach loses its last firmness. As you read,
a skirt falls to a bedroom floor, tires crush
a crawling animal, fingers press piano keys.
What happens during a pause in your talk
could keep you typing until your last breath. Always
a bullet leaves a gun, honey pours from a spoon.
Your brain is a mussel shell that will never hold the ocean.

Tim Bowling

Tim Bowling(1964-) was born in Vancouver, BC, and raised in the nearby town of Ladner. He has published three collections of poems—*Low Water Slack*, *Dying Scarlet*, and *The Thin Smoke of the Heart*—and one novel—*The Downriver Drift*. He lives in Edmonton, Alberta.

Spectrum

In Ireland, I ran up a steep hill to try to prove my youth,
but green defeated me, green laid me down, green wrapped
my body in its Irish embrace, and laid it, breathless,
down.

On the Fraser River, I took the lives of salmon to try to live my own,
but silver defeated me, silver laid me down, silver touched
my body with fleet kisses, and laid it, trembling,
down.

It took your blue eyes to teach me how the colours always win,
and how in their winning is our victory; again and again,
in every way, your blue defeats me, your blue lays me down,
your blue caresses my body, and lays it, as on green grasses,
as in silver schools, rapturously, rapturously,
down.

Family Bible

*for my grandmother, Margaret Stevens (1881-1945), and her
children, the three living and the fourteen dead*

My totem is black as the rains of Haida Gwaii; black
is my totem with tears of generations, a burnt block
of cedar sinewed with Latinate phrases and names
of dead infants tallied each year to poverty's pox
and polio; my totem is black and keeps a Christ
in its grain, His words, His blood, and His high cross;
black is my totem and the eyes that raised it, from
bedside tables to parlours of grief; my totem is black
and lurid with the ink of an illiterate hand, mother
to Toronto's graves, daughter to a dashed Irish dream;
black is my totem as the winter rains of Haida Gwaii.

Let the spiders nest in the rot of its wood, in
the soft pit of faith that sways in the wind,
under the garish streak of the mask of pain,
under the slash of light, that naked bulb
above the childbirth-bed, cast on the three
sets of twins uncried at the slap, cast on
the multiple coughs in the crib, cast on
the woman whose body is rain, and rains
through her days, her months, and her years.

Let the crows light and caw, let them sound
out the storms of the steaming kettles
that filled her kitchen as she inked the pages
and hummed the hymns, let their black wings
wreathe the rented door while the undertaker
takes her teenaged girl unprettied to her
piece of earth. Let my totem eat the storm,
black into the burnt block, rain into char;
let it suffer the names of the little children
in a night without stars, as she did, turning
tear-streaked again to her husband's warmth.

Then let the sun break red over Haida Gwaii.

A Small Essay in Honour of the Past

The soul of a journey is liberty, perfect liberty, to
think, feel, do just as one pleases. We go a journey
chiefly to be free of all impediments, and of all
inconveniences, to leave ourselves behind.

William Hazlitt

For just one night, to be William Hazlitt
going a journey at the end of the eighteenth century,
deliciously alone on the road to some walled and turreted
town with a Hog's Head Inn and amber lamplight puddling the gloom.
To anticipate steaming viands and whole goblets of tea and a long
repose with a letter carried with me from London. To recite
as I stroll some favourite lines by my good friend, Coleridge,
something about green upland swells and bleating flocks. To own
my mind in a solitude so pure only a bottle of sherry and
a cold chicken could bring me back to the physical world.
Is it too much to want this, for just one night, at the end
of the twentieth century? A few quiet hours on a narrow road
lit by stars? A groom whispering tender praise to my fatigue
as he leads it to the stable? The Irish setter of a fire curled
at my feet, growling at my one foe, worry, in his sleep?
Somewhere the ghost of Hazlitt approaches an old village
at nightfall, delighting in dreams of onion-smothered rabbit.
He refuses to believe his lips are cold and that the Host
of the Hog's Head will not take his useless coins. I love
his obstinance in the face of death. O for just one night,
to be the warm body supping pleasure in his wake.

Lucy Brennan

Lucy Brennan (1931-) was born in Dublin, Ireland, and now lives in Whitby, Ontario. Her poetry has appeared in many Canadian and overseas publications. Her collection, *Migrants All*, was published in 1999 and she is included in *The White Page/An Bhileog Bhán—Twentieth Century Irish Women Poets*.

Sweeney and the Scholars

"But you must exist," pondered Bernard Lonergan,
late of Toronto's Regis College,
"because of her inherited imagination:
if you functioned as a myth,
you would go no further than all myth,
and be but a faint clue to the absolute."
"The Absolute!" interrupted John Scotus Eriugena,
late of the Court of Charles the Bald.
"They say I have a passion for the Absolute!"
"But that seems absurd!" murmured
Samuel Beckett, late of Paris,
as he engaged the argument.

And Sweeney smiled and scratched
between the feathers on his shoulders.

"Your expertise is generated
in your intricate, inverted Irish minds.
Now tell me all you three
why I still exist—whether in word
or on hard earth is nowhere relevant.
Centuries have passed and yet I'm known
to minds like yours and no less
to the children who delight
in sad and monstrous creatures.
Tell what keeps me here."

"You are a symbol of pride before a fall."
"And after, don't forget. It isn't pride
that keeps me going now."
"You are a way of reconciling and accepting
disorder into order,
of making sensible the senseless."

"You are the human who borders
on the inhuman—the man
whom inhumanity declares an outcast."

"You are an insight!"
                              "Unreal!"
"Irreconcilable!"
                              Sweeney laughed: "And everlasting!"
and left them to their discourse,
in which, as in most Irish argument,
the scholars' points of view
turn round as many times as there are scholars.

Betwixt and Between

> Sweeney went mad and took to the air,
> like a bird, in fulfillment of Ronan's curse.

To-day I am Sweeney's hag:
I bear him the itch of questions
about the eerie mist, the incessant waves,
the land he flounders over,
and whether the shape of a stone
in the fingers matters.

Cursed, proud Sweeney turned
into a winged itinerant
driven with the clouds.
Now, like a stunt-man, bird-man,
he clings outside my window,
presses his face to the glass of my speeding train.

Where will you wander to-day? I ask.
What child will you talk to
or what wild spirit will you woo?
Will you find me again this evening
when out of the brooding dark
a slant moon peers?

Sweeney, you trail centuries,
while I move through minutes.
Can you tell me what death is,
that comes in a second?
I ride him with questions.
Surely we live on the riddle's rim?

Anne Compton

Anne Compton (1947-), poet and critic, was born on Prince Edward Island, the eleventh child in a family of eleven. She is the author of *A.J.M. Smith: Canadian Metaphysical*. Her poems appear in Canadian and American journals.

Lightwork in Vermeer

No one knows why the light in Delft is different from everywhere
nor why the women in Vermeer stitch and pour, make lace and music,
write and receive letters   weigh air
in concentrated stillness.

And though the critic remarks, "the restrictive ordinariness
of his subject matter," meaning the women's work, where but here,
"in two smallish rooms," might miracle occur?

The windows of Vermeer open inward
letting eternity flow over a sill
in parody of earthlight.

Not earthly, at all, the dispersal of light
that through a north-facing window retrieves
The Milkmaid from time, ennobles
the bread, the jug, and the wicker. Converts
the fluid to forever.

In almost every painting (in all, fewer than forty)
the women, gentle and disbelieving, turn to us,
"You did not know," they say or will say:
the spoken and the unspoken being the same in this light.

They wear their vestments—lemony yellow, ultramarine blue—
like stonework. These women who cannot age.
The merit of pearls is theirs also: touches of opalescent white
    without outline.

The Woman with the Scales ignores the pearls scattered before her
—a lapidary lapse brought on by light
her uplifted arm welcomes
the heft of light on her limbs
weighable radiance
the illuminated white of the hood and the smock enfold her
away.

In the viscid air, the gestures of the women slow and halt,
become masonry.

By the windows of Vermeer, light is suspensive.

The Mermaids Singing

Dear Mr. Prufrock, could you manage tea Wednesday week.
It is the shuttered house on the hill where the road curves.
I believe you've been (nearby) before.
Cousin Frances, the lepidopterist, is with us for the month;
of course, she hasn't brought the collection
but she loves to talk. Some say she's sibyllic.
The usual, including Bixie and Freddie, will be here.
Mind the dogs on the stair as you approach (Daddy
is so silly about the dogs since he bought that disagreeable little
    drawing, *Salome.*)
They'll drag the least thing down: *ungart'red, and down-gyved to
    his ankle*—all's bear.
I hope you'll be firm. Yours, Cordelia Merman.

Unreadable Flowers

When Catherine Parr Traill met Ophelia at the brookside
she gave the brooding naturalist a talking-to.
Your alphabet of flowers, my good girl,
will not spell here. It's a cold climate.
Serviceable shoes and notions, that's what's wanted here.
Sensibility tends to derangement and aimless
wandering. Not so long ago, Fancy starved here
for just that reason
though flowers—edible in all shades but yellow—make
"marvellous food" and serve sundry uses, as for instance:
the stamen of the *Ranunculaceae* is long and hooded
[very forward, you can't miss it]
its pollen, if carefully collected, yields a prophylactic.
In spring, the root—of Monkshood or nun's habit—
    prevents conception.
Although for this, proper footwear will serve.
Also good for wading.

Marlene Cookshaw

Marlene Cookshaw (1953-) was born in Lethbridge, Alberta, and has lived on the west coast of BC since 1980. Her most recent collection of poems is *Double Somersaults*. Earlier books include *The Whole Elephant* and *Coupling*. She lives on Pender Island and is editor of *The Malahat Review*.

What the Brain Tells the Body When He Enters the Room

I give over. I give up. You want the world.
Leave me out. Forget the way home. You want

the world on your tongue. Don't look
at your watch. Open your mouth, which believes

it will never be night. The second hand indicates
nothing, reiterates merely the rift between wanting

and having. Ask. Ask again. Little
ragged flower, bud-nipped, triumphant.

Have I said, Among weeds? Have I said, Yellow?
What do I know of this except what

over the edge is? Open your legs. Lose
even the meaning of home. Soon.

Or you will be sick with cigarettes, caffeine
and longing. Already you're undone, and proud of it.

Planetesimal

Farthest planet, Pluto, from the heart, though
not always, its orbit severely

elliptic, estrangement from the sun
sometimes thirty, sometimes fifty that of Earth's.

All cycles are delicate, of course, all threaten
to cease repeating, to swing

into an orbit so far from circular
nothing can be counted on. These things

happen. Like snow. The chickens hate it,
the snow, which lights up the night.

The rooster screams at it, the pullet
looks confused, the hen determined.

Pluto is barely two-thirds of our moon,
and winter's 124 years long. Uncharted

when my parents were young,
the universe was smaller, less detailed.

What can numbers teach us anyway? Proportion,
a little. Eventually. Pluto has

its own moon, revealed only
the year I left the glacier-scraped prairie

with my dog, for the green place
where mountains reared up from the sea.

Charon is half the size of Pluto. They
are really twin planets, rock and ice,

planetesimals, adolescent, unfinished
as Earth when flung out from the sun.

Unwanted and eloquent as snow in late spring.
It falls again in this season, soft and heavy

as a child's eyelids, as memory, as down
the hen herself has plucked to line the nest.

————————

Nice Girls

don't sit like that.
She says. We are

to keep our knees together,
ask no energy from earth,

we are to circle it:
small planets, moons

in aprons. So. Legs angled
obliquely, we

orbit. A mother denies her daughters
a firm grip on the earth.

Satellites. Withdrawn. Unstable.
The gravity of this eludes her.

Afua Cooper

Afua Cooper (1957-) was born in Westmoreland, Jamaica. She grew up in Kingston, Jamaica, and migrated to Canada in 1980. She has published four books of poetry and completed a PhD in African-Canadian history at the University of Toronto.

Fire Woman II

Old Women
(perhaps from Danhomé)
crept into my house dressed in robes of crimson
and breathed upon me their breath of fire
they took charge of my house,
painted its walls red
(this caused the unwanted occupants to flee).
Then they gave me a fire bath
(said it would make me invincible)
For my sustenance, they fed me grapes
(from Mary's vineyard)
the juice of which warmed my blood
and caused me to utter in scarlet tongues
For my birthday, they gave me live coals
then changed my name to Ruby

My Illusion

That we run away to Portland
in the mountains
to a place called House Hill
where you can touch heaven with your finger
and each morning awakened by rain drizzling
thru a rainbowed sunlight
there you can stand on your own peak
and see the lighthouse at Port Morant
sending signs to voyagers
and on a clear day
see the outline of Cuba
Oriente, Oriente

Or it could be Port Antonio
the side where the land juts
into the sea
close to the lagoon
every day we would feast on mangos and mint tea
and make love in the purple air of twilight

It was in Portland by the Blue Lagoon
that I saw the brightest moon
rose from the black sea
and strode naked across the sky
conquering all with her luminous light

Night Ease

Grandmothers carried loads on their heads
babies in their arms
men in their hearts
cut sugarcane until their palms became calloused and bruised,
their backs bent, neck stiff, spines mis-shapen and a permanent
    hurt lodged
itself in their shoulders
grandmas want to lay their burden down
by the riverside

Grandmothers now lose all dem teeth
but in their mouths are dutty tuff stories
making bread outta stone stories
and stories of how they made it to the other side
of how time pass
an di children grow
an di men die
an the hurt ease
as evening brings with it, its purple peace

Now
grandmas sit by their doorstep gazing onto the street
seated in themselves
smoking their pipes
oracling the scene

Mary Dalton (1950-) lives in St. John's, Newfoundland, and teaches at Memorial University. She has published two collections of poetry, *The Time of Icicles*, 1989, and, *Allowing the Light*, 1993. The poems included here are part of a series, "The Tall World of Their Torn Stories," inspired by Newfoundland speech.

Mary Dalton

The Tall World of Their Torn Stories

1   Jesus and His Gashes

You'd go on tiptoe, I'll guarantee you
That—Jesus and his gashes
Everywhere you laid your eyes.
His bleeding heart, its bracelet
Of thorns, red gleams in the hall.
In the parlour he hung limp
From the cross, white as
The halibut, the wounds
In his side, the sponge
Dipped in vinegar.
Nights his sloe eyes
Swam up through the kelp.
The salt cod, cruciform,
The shape of our days.

2   Flirrup

Fairy squalls on the water.
I'm marooned at the window,
Waiting for the fog man,
Sewing the old black veil.
The walls of Troy on the floor.
There's Dickey just gone up
The road in a red shirt. He's
Sure not the fog man—

Traipsing along with the swagger
Of a swiler in the spring fat.
Not a feather out of him.
Now he'd be the one to have in
For a feed of fresh flippers,
A taste of my fine figgy cake.

3   Elt

He'd the face of a robber's horse.
And he'd drink the rum off the dead Nelson.
Any devilment, he was sure to be in it, right
Up to his face and eyes.
When he danced in the halls, there was a fine
Chance of a fierce racket before the night was over.
Once that mawmouth talked my young Eileen
Out by the river to watch the merry dancers.
An idler, a twister, an outright slieveen.
His mother was a moonlight child;
His father a moonshiner.

4   Water Pups

On shore, to think on the water.
Once out, windshook as a rotten pine,
To see in sleep the great water bears
And go in dread of a wild weather light,
To burn with the fire of water pups—
Hands full right up to the elbow—
Sometimes so big two'd go into one.
To think on the yoked goats,
The rocky paths, the rum
Puncheon's gurgle, the spout of
The yellowbelly, junks-a-crackle in the red stove,
The missus and youngsters run down from the flake.
Out on the water, to think on the shore.

Burn

1   When the saltwater burns—
    Cities tumbling pillars in
    Sheets of flame on the water—
    It's sure to be a south wind
    And massing thick with fish.

2   A thin line a good salter walks—
    Salt his man or his master.
    Not enough salt makes the fish greasy,
    Slippery, too slimy to dry.
    Too much salt burns up the fish—
    All brittle when it comes to dry.

3   Nothing in him but bung-your-eye—
    He walked ten miles in the blizzard—
    The frost burnt his toes—
    Thawed by the fire, they
    Mortified so far that off came
    The nails, and bared the ends of his bones.
    And all he could talk of was the kentals of cod.

Lynn Davies

Lynn Davies'(1954-) non-fiction has appeared in many Canadian magazines and her stories for children have been published in various anthologies. She has been awarded a scholarship to the Banff Centre for the Arts and the Lina Chartrand Poetry Award. Her first book, *The Bridge That Carries the Road*, was nominated for the 1999 Governor General's Award for Poetry. Lynn lives with her family on McLeod Hill, New Brunswick.

The Cherry Tree

A distant train reminds me of other journeys
I've taken. A whistle pulling me towards
a family stunned by death's abrupt arrival.
And once, my daughter and I, through dark hills
pulsing with fireflies and heat lightning,
her brother beginning to fill my belly. Now
the applause of rain on leaves adds up our days.
Eases off, a tip-tapping, bountiful murmur.
When it stops, the neighbourhood kids
and blue jays come to strip our tree of cherries.
Sudden ammunition, how to spit a pit at a friend.
Wings flapping, raucous squawking, over the fruit
and green leafage. Who can argue with sequence?
White blossoms, then the cherries, now these appetites.

Cape Enrage

Only a picture from a blue tin box.
                                    The day
we shared lunch on a blanket over stones, my mother
pouring from a thermos, steam curling like smoke,
the cocoa dark as the Fundy tide relinquishing the flats,
        exposed mud shiny as a giant's mirror.
My footprints trekking through clouds and sky,
searching for the spot where the tide turns.

                                    In the picture
I wear the moss green jacket my mother sewed for me.
Hold my father's hand under a cliff, in the cave
he told me never dried out between tides.
Then the slow drive down a dirt road so narrow
        we had to shut windows to keep out the leaves,
        frantic as trapped insects against the glass.
Onto the lined, somnolent pavement
leading inland to bed where I lay thinking
of that cave full of ocean,
all entrance gone.

Hartlen Point

As I pick up what the hurricane tore off our trees,
I think of the drive to see the storm's surf
        pound Hartlen Point last night.
How my son and I watched our friends trudge
into the wind and rain that shook our car
in the darkness. A circus ride he
wanted to stop and get off. Go home.

We talked of dinosaurs as big as this storm,
and the comet we saw last spring, just left
of the Big Dipper's handle. Out here, away
from city lights, the reluctant fingerprint
of a traveller not wanting company. My son
wondered where the comet could be now, how far
        it might go before it collides
with a ringed planet. I thought how close
it came to never entering our sight at all.

Now I store winter kindling, curse the cat
who brought home the cedar waxwing.
The bird who survived last night's storm
        tossed broken on our driveway.
The body ripped open, the pavement
stained with blood bright as red currants,
        place names on a map.

Iain Deans

Iain Deans (1973-) was born in Montreal and lives in Halifax, Nova Scotia, where he works as a copywriter. He graduated from Queen's University with a BA in History. Iain's work has appeared in a number of magazines across the country.

This Spider like a Hand

This spider like a hand with fingers spread
a palm searching,

this web a place a vision spun a song
in thin string.   Spreading across branches
of flexible physics,

a growing place   a space between thoughts.

This hand
with fingers spread waves itself across
growth and
status

                     this is the spider this hand
this constant hello of fingers
this fascination with balance

                          and threads like thought.

Insects

I am making you a wedding ring in the form of a mathematical equation. I have been scratching out the numbers and symbols with India ink. My movements across the page have been like the short thrusts and stabs of an insect.

The formula is based on the solution to Fermat's Theorem. That solution required the invention of whole new systems of mathematics.

Like our union, it can only exist on a highly abstract plane. Like the ballet of angry horseflies. Like the art of thousand-year-old millipedes pulling an army of appendages across the sand. Or the percussive music of cockroach feet on linoleum floors.

The formula is partially hinged on the existence of imaginary numbers. Like i. Lowercase, and forever trapped by cummings. Like me. Imaginary numbers for a lover I am bound to on paper. Letters, back and forth. In this letter a formula. A proposal in abstract. In yours a reply.

And so on.

If you answer yes, I will trace the formula on your right breast with an ant leg dipped in ink.

When we make love, we will be transported into the realm of applied theory.

And insects.

From the Mantelpiece a Message

The stone Buddha you gave me gets up,
lotus freed knees shaking off dust and

now ready to float, but instead a pause
to breathe in the wow of it all and

I'm frozen in my chair when
he says your name beach sand smooth

reaches me on powdery feet, rough fingers
clink against teacups, expresses

an interest in the exchange of notes so that
we may better paint the you who

passed through us both when you thought I
needed a guardian, and he needed a home

you should know that we are both
satisfied with the arrangement

we have signals to send you
look for our faces everywhere

Jeffery Donaldson

Jeffery Donaldson (1960-) was born
and raised in Toronto, educated at
Victoria College, University of
Toronto, and now teaches poetry at
McMaster University. He lives in
Hamilton with his wife Annette Abma
and children Miller and Cornelia.

Feddy Doe

"Cooshay and feddy doe: Up the wooden stair
and to sleep." I can hear my father's voice.
Each night at the bedtime hour he was there,

sent these words behind me to the house top.
It was really a parqueted tile floor
that angled up in gyres through our low-rent

suburban townhouse to the room above.
And I was Orpheus the wrong way round,
climbing from the dream spaces of a life

in time—the flickering tv firelights,
the thread of conversation my mother
would needle from her mending—to the sheer

underworld's upper sphere, fallen to shades
beyond the landing, where my own raised spirit
each time followed to a point, and though

I turned round more than once, just disappeared.
But his words were mild and palliative,
so "Cooshay and feddy doe," I replied,

feeling that often, with no stronger spell
to ward off chimeras I knew were there,
a home-made incantation worked as well.

And chimed "up the wooden stair and to sleep..."
For that was what they meant, the cryptic sounds,
my father said. Two ways to put the same thing.

The magic part was French Canadian,
that much I knew. As for the English half,
I had to follow through it to the end

in no uncertain terms, and at his word,
the cold blank stair went up in the dark
farther than I could see, and though I felt

that a terror of it was beneath me,
I sensed a jittered railing under grip,
and noiselessly held onto it, the thought

of where it led me growing clear, by steps
more bewildering, like a nightfall's
gradually distincter star on star.

My room was all dark forms and outlines,
the closet and the drapes in mock charade
moved when I moved, and always faced me square.

When I turned, the bed was ten miles away.
There was an oblong window of moonlight
on the floor, and beside it a chair,

and in the chair, propped like a tippler
bunched up under his own weight, my father's
oak-carved, antique marionette looked out.

Cuttings of sun-browned curtain for a suit
patched with neat squares of a checkered dish-cloth.
One leg was off. All up in arms with string.

Its face was painted like a tart's, red cheeks,
red lips, hysteric smile, and oak-hard stare
that returned the blank appearances in kind

of whatever it saw there in the dark.
I didn't see, for each night what brought me
to my senses with a shake was the gaze

itself, impenetrable, *laissez faire,*
whose point I only later understood.
You start seeing things if you close your eyes.

Cooshay and feddy doe. As I grew up,
I felt the same need to trade the mystic
theatre of the word for cause, effect.

By the time I heard *coucher* in first-year
French, I was only just learning to lie
down among half truths, and wanted the rest.

But *feddy doe?*...how would I get from there
to *wooden steps* in French? I didn't know.
And then one night, a movie on tv,

a woman sees her daughter off to bed,
reads to her from a book until she sleeps,
kisses her brow good night. "Fais de beaux rêves,"

she whispers in her ear. And I saw a child,
with closed eyes, long gone for a sweeter dream,
lost in translation on the wooden stair.

John Donlan

John Donlan (1944-) was raised in Baysville, Ontario, and lives in Vancouver, BC, where he works as a reference librarian at the Vancouver Public Library, and poetry editor with Brick Books. He is the author of three books of poetry; his most recent, *Green Man*, was published in 1999.

Mirage

What lives below tears comes to light again
—like your near-dying; around your bed the pious
doctors, the family hardly believing, numb,
and you calm, as whiteness almost overwhelmed you.

It racks you to return to the fever
and ache of wanting, to let go of the tough
survival mode of soldiers: mustn't they erase
almost everything so they don't go mad

comparing their old lives with war?
They keep for themselves only one or two truths—
some early Eden, a clean weapon.
Fear's rigid armour holds their breath

hostage, without making them bulletproof.
Waiting through the worst, they burn their will
like cigarettes. Some nights they still snap
awake, not breathing, years after peace breaks out.

Picture

for Gary Brownlee

They were wild childhoods
beside the swamp: half-animal, we ventured
deeper where roots lifted their knees
from dark ponds further darkened where our fathers
had poured crankcase oil.

Up on Church Hill big kids threatened
to cut off our dicks unless we'd run
so they could hunt us with pellet guns. A slug
hit Gab over the eye. They let us go
if we'd lie for them. We had stonefights

in the gravel pits: missiles whirred
thrillingly near our heads like hummingbirds.
We all remember. Betty hanged
herself while her baby cried. No one knew how
to stop. Stop the picture.

26 September 1994

Tilt

Dear body, snow fell many miles
as if to be with you today.
The river with its ruff of ice reminds you
to protect the warm column of blood
around your voice—the voice you sometimes feel
there is no use for.
Dear body, the birds have voices, don't they?
So let's not have any more nonsense of that sort.

You love surface geology: here—
take this slope anchored in pines and grasses,
this jacked-up slab of crumbling sea-floor we call Mountain;
wear the earth as if it was your skin.
Don't forget you have that wet red muscle
pushing heat to your limits, dear body,
beyond any extremity you know.

31 October 1995

jodi essery

Originally from Kenora, Ontario, jodi essery (1975-) graduated from the Drama Program at Queen's University and now teaches English and Drama in Toronto. Her poems and short stories have appeared in journals and magazines in Canada, and *Contact Listenings: Kingston Poetry and Prose*.

dog

for lager

i.
a bristled tide you rush
the corners
of this small apartment
my careful markers of territory
insufficient buoys caught
in a wake of tail

dispensing with formality you move straight to the toilet

ii.
all day you push the walls
with your desperate testimony
hoarse with a fervent evangelism
that dams each attempt to contain you

by nightfall, nothing is sacred
even the garbage has spilled its dark secrets to you
tampon condom old cheese

iii.
spent with the labour of longing
we retreat

to lick our separate wounds
searching the salt of our lost master

how long since we have eaten?
how long since we have been outside?

iv.
and your overturned water bowl
drowns our last straggled pretensions

nosing into the bathroom to nudge me
naked and unsure
before you

married in our mistrust of everything
outside this room
we take our meals on the kitchen floor

at night
hold each other in sleep
tangled mess of hair and ears

lovers of a new order

v.
these are secrets we pass between us
even after he has returned

still life with pomegranate

i.

the way he is transfixed by
the fruit her meticulous
attention to the rough skin; held
by the exotic shape and oh! the spill
of seeds into the bowl his eyes
following the burst seed spreading
into her sweater like a blush like
a small and unexpected wound

ii.

the way he leans towards
her asking for a pen for
tea forgiveness the small
ascension at the end of
things the halved moon laying
between them on the pillow

iii.

the way they have both dreamed of vienna

iv.

the way the room holds
its silence the morning slow
sudden sun breaking
across the carpet a huge
and blinding wave day
returning to itself

v.

the way they remember
details fruit pen
subtle gesture of moon

Colleen Flood

Colleen Flood (1953-) was born in Sault Ste. Marie, Ontario, lives in Toronto and has two daughters. She has published poems in numerous journals across Canada and her first collection of poems, *Bonding with Gravity*, was published in 1998.

Mormon Square Dancers

Who has more fun
than Mormon square dancers?
Configured in Cartesian symmetry
of gingham daisy chains and circling bees.
Seen from on high, a floral tapestry
of pastel swirls, a pleasing choreography.
Now swing your girls!

Each tiered skirt partnered to
a checkered shirt; they mate for life
and all eternity, clasped like the two ends of a bolo tie.
From square one, God laid out the plan when
Male and Female made He them:
Left allemande, Step high!
Now go forth, Do-si-do
and Multiply!

They heed the call, they're led
by Seers, they trace their lineage
to the pioneers.
Strait is the gate, and narrow too,
but faithful Mormons Dj-ive through.
Dodging Injuns, Hand over hand,
all Promenade to the Promised Land—
pausing on the way for Western sandwiches!

God said to His Dancers:
Fast and Pray!
Repent and Right sashay!
Commands so rapid-fire and technical
that most of us fall by the way...
It's healthy sweat and good clean fun
and when this Earthly set is done,
beyond the pull of the turning world
Celestial dancers
Spin and whirl.

What!

stark as Earth's end
forces our eyes up
to crest the knoll of Fall

blazing shaft of foliage
rises contra blue to flaunt
its dying in our faces

sucks red out of sunset
fingers taut   veins stopped
in one cold snap

swelling chromatic strain
of bronze and cobalt
exultation

to startle us right out
of downcast mutterings
and footfall's plodding

pillar of light we
doubting   touch
and pile up words

like stones to meet
your vaunting height
overarching all

our shining sorrow

Albert Fuller

Albert Fuller (1954-) was born in Trinidad and Tobago, educated in North America, and currently resides in Toronto. He is a member of the League of Canadian Poets and his collection, *flowers in the empty house*, was published in 1998.

children who hunger for space

there are reticent children whose mouths speak of silence
whose eyes become watchful in the presence of adults
children who are dreams known only to themselves
who are all the Wednesdays that have been forgotten

there are children whose beliefs breathe in the old stories
who are a fire
who like sailors take on an incredible journey
that passes beyond the rim of the world—
these children who have gone looking for promises
who search amidst the cracks of the sea

alone   they whisper among themselves
with none to guess the vast extent of darkness they must taste
a burden of longing that is the blood of their eyes:
these are the children who believe in what lives
beyond the end of the corridor
that there is a sunlight waiting to enter their eyes
a spaciousness wanting their touch
a secret to be unfolded like a vast landscape

"the day passes..."

the day passes
             like a figure
too big for the perspective delineated
on a canvas washed with a blue background
and geraniums that run wild
        with fierce hot colour

from behind a window
a woman in yesterday's clothes reads a book of fiction
she finds the essential woman   an Emily Brontë   in herself
unmoored amidst dirty teacups and
a brutally oppressive hernia of smiles

behind her eyelids
there is a languishing winter night
and a dying that comes
from every flake of falling snow

The Apollinaire Apartments

the parking lot is a sea of colour
leaves falling indifferently on the surface of things
then sailing off to decompose into the soil

people coming here are a signature of sounds
a clutter of disconnected reminiscences
taking vehicles that fade into a shining traffic

I foretell a car will pull in swiftly and stop in an abrupt silence
a young woman will walk across the parking lot and become invisible
going into the white building

Mary Elizabeth Grace

Mary Elizabeth Grace (1965-) was born in Burks Falls, Ontario, and lives in Montreal. Author of the book and companion CD, *Bootlegging Apples on the Road to Redemption*, she has also been published in numerous anthologies and two, four-author collections, *Mad Angels and Amphetamines* and *Crossroads Cant*.

So May You

So may you lay beside me loved one
and be tender,
trace the lines etched into my face

tell me,
no promise,
all of it means art not ending

So may you stand beside me loved one
and be faith,
notice the shapes and shadows

tell me,
no promise,
one can always know a painter
by the mixing of her greys

Shades of Yellow

I want to buy you sunflowers, all I can afford are
seeds. I want to give you for all the shades of
yellow you bring to me. So I go to the grocery
store, buy six lemons, paint on happy faces, leave
them, there on the kitchen table. I come home,
it's late, there is no furniture, there are no walls.
I'm standing in a summer field, sweet corn
undressed.

late september pear

She said,
but is his voice music to you

I said
his skin is the sweet of late september pear

yes, but is his voice music to you

I said, his skin is the sweet of
late september pear, and kissing him
is like kissing silence and if
music is very, very, very good at
the very end you can feel
it's silence inside your body.

Carla Hartsfield

Carla Hartsfield (1956-) was born in Waxahachie, Texas, and immigrated to Canada in 1982. She is a classically-trained musician and songwriter who has published two collections of poetry. Her most recent book, *Fire Never Sleeps*, has been added to the Sylvia Plath Archives at Smith College.

Meeting Leon Fleischer
at the Corner of Bedford & Bloor

I like to think it was unavoidable,
just like playing K. 570 for him
at the University of Texas. Or fated,

as one of Fleischer's surgeries,
the scars notated onto his right hand,
clearly spelling out unlucky.

A spirit above skates the twilight moon.
And I see Schubert on the flip side,
with a pockmarked face like a driving range.

For the second time in my life
I'm poised at some kind of precipice
with Leon Fleischer, light beginning

to sing "The Wanderer Fantasy."
We're both coming back
to the conservatory from dinner,

and Leon looks formidable
with his tousled hair and woollen scarf,
as if the years of conducting,

of cradling that hand close to his body,
might be worth recording pieces
composed for World War I vets

with shot-off right arms.
Thank God for Ravel.
Thank God for Scriabin.

Though, Fleischer isn't alone.
Many musicians, including myself,
have been lured into nine feet

of glistening, black chasm, where
the only music that plays
is blood trying to course

through nerve-damaged fingers.
Instead we chat, Leon and I.
He thinks he remembers my clean

but homegrown version of Mozart.
"Your face is not unfamiliar,"
he booms politely—Schubert,

the wingless apparition, stands
briefly between his shoulders,
a chorus of nightsky flooding

Varsity Stadium. Even before
he unwinds that surgery-ridden hand
to say goodbye, I'm sure I've never seen

anything like it. With mine locked into his,
we fly to our studios without aid
of limbs or instruments;

no need to wait for the go-ahead signal
at the corner of Bedford and Bloor;
there are other ways to continue,

nonetheless. .

Playing

Learning to love you is a little
like playing the piano in the dark. My fingers
feel for narrow crevices, carry me
into pianissimos where bone
was at first imperceptible.

I played the piano once, you said,
singing your fingers over my body,
glissando. And rain!
Coating the streets with silver—
soon find its lens
floating over us.
           And I imagine
our damp bodies lifted out of
this night-window, a piano's black water;
the two of us lying in the streets
sheened as pocket mirrors,
wet and cool with no other need
than to reflect each other.
           As for your body now,
playing into the white, slim edges
of mine, it feels all so new,
so perfect and new, I want to show you
those mirrors of rain
twirling through August,
their deep corridors rushing
to that hollow of the body: my heart,
the dark, dry chamber.

Merike Lugus

Merike Lugus (1943-) was born in Estonia and spent her early years in Germany and Sweden. She took a long route to writing, through an MA in sociology, and through years of painting and sculpting. Her first book of poetry, *Ophelia After Centuries of Trying*, was published in 1998. She is currently at work on a novel and a collection of short stories. She lives near Cobourg, Ontario, in the hills of Northumberland.

Glass Fragment

Is it just a piece of something
we once called a vase,
a reminder of a careless stunt,
a broken thing
briefly mourned and forgotten?
or is it a bolt out of blueness,
an instance of ultramarine
in itself complete?

This quiet morning demands
absolutely nothing
mind drifts to
inviolable places—
a dove's astounded eye
a child's Achilles' heel
then to the fragment placed with care
against the window pane

Blueness is firm
and does not yield to further fragmentation
or to perfecting by the mind's rasp
light pours in and settles on
the southern shore of Blue
like a colony of diamonds
briefly, before dispersal

Knowing

where the grass quivers
a small body slips into the green
thickets of our minds
existence somewhere has shifted
or someone somewhere
is arriving or has gone away
all we are left with is the knowing
that something must be done

sometimes we are children
our ears pressed to conches
we eavesdrop on ancient wisdom
defer to mystery as the deepest answer
but sometimes we start at the beginning
drawing the boundaries:
this must be you, this is me,
this is love, and this, invasion

again a tiny shift, ripples of light
along the fragile seed heads
the grass at the parting quivers
and all at once the aspect
of the field has changed

or else we never were
where we thought we'd been—
we really can't remember
standing anywhere but here
or how it felt not knowng
the thing that must be done

Fury in Search of Cause

swelling to titan size I look down
at your excuses so foolishly peeled—
look up, see my mammoth boulder
set in motion—you have no option now but
to feel the earth tremble
and to inquire how it all began
how we fell like two leaves into the same current

anything to bust the dam
come swirling down the mountain
froth and fury needing to crash against
youthful and upright truth
later we will speak of
damage control
this is also relevant to how this morning I was
filled with joyous recognition
looking at this tree, that travelling sky
knowing there are journeys and always people
lurching forward or engaged in
some odd sort of dance

at the moment I am feeling someone's death
too many trains passing by carrying the dead
and me under the bridge hunched like a troll
brooding on the word *home*
I shiver
shouldn't someone keep count and weep?
and so I whimper, but dishonestly, because
what I'm really recollecting is
how yesterday you did not call

Eric Miller

Eric Miller (1961-) was born in Toronto and lives in Dartmouth, Nova Scotia. His book of prose and poetry, *Song of the Vulgar Starling*, appeared in 1999, and his poetry won the Academy of American Poets Prize in 1996.

A Baby's Bent Head

Pensive as a boulder, the volume of thought
perfectly flush with the dome of its idea,
flossy over the scalp with light growing
indistinguishably from hair—
hair and light one indisseverable filament—,
moss of infant incandescence across mild rock,
preposterous maturity as though
a bud might rightly succeed a blown flower,
concentration as relaxation,
bone and flesh sibling in softness
and the brow frownlessly profound in its meditation,
this head, drooping, exerts a pull on our esteem
as though to bend the world's precocious petals
around its compression, obliging
obeisance to its simple inclination,
a half-nod bottomless like a god's
though wet, perennially, with snail-dawdle
of drool which haltingly drips and
stickily like a primordial water-clock
whose stalactite ought to, but doesn't form.

Night Park

As cyclonic swifts focus their horde
on the exiguous chimney of their night roost,
vacillating satellites hostage to
the psychomachia of Sun and Moon
and oblivion sucks down just one at a time,
the rest defiant as though to suspend sleep
signified a moral victory and the sustained
temptation to fall were already identical with
the triumph of virtue (temptation being the most
inexhaustible engine, a *perpetuum mobile*
planing the skyline like a circular saw),
and fatigue's casualties flake from the vortical
orbit, excommunicated from the circuitous cult
of the visible like the chlorotic rays of the Sun—

so around the clipped dictates of the boxwood hedges
and around the superbly standing wave of the housefronts,
around the phragmites shivering by the pond
like nakedness excited or cold nakedness for sale,
around the loosestrife lanterns and the gilt
adornment flaking from black water,
around the mallard ducks' fear—concentrics
flexing out from plump hulls of misgiving—,
and around the hortensia browning in its urn
(blighted petals like the bruises of the rest),
and around the intenser nights long since roosting
in clenched trees that keep their eclipse like jealous gods,

ignorant Lust goes spinning nightly,
a rowboat that pivots on a single oar,
a bird that gyrates on one broken wing,
pressed always forward by limbo's brood of options
(launch, they cry, oh launch the formation of the future's body)—
but Lust finds children quite inconceivable

though it may pace nightly around the wrought-iron playground staves
and around the cement coast of the circular wading pool
and the simple carousel propelled by hand—

Lust cannot learn, it only swerves;
eyes flash tossing on its cruising rim,
it twists on the heel of its vicious circle,
it banks blackly as a swift deferring the narrow way to sleep;

and when it succumbs, it will have burst into tomorrow
and from a tall roost the dawn wanderers will disperse
having gestated the night,

leaving not in circles but in tangents
of some more wayward and more genial manifestation of desire.

Lyle Neff

Lyle Neff (1969-) was born in Prince George, British Columbia, and currently lives and works in Vancouver. His first book, *Ivanhoe Station*, published in 1997, was nominated for the Dorothy Livesay Prize at the BC Book Awards. His next book, *Full Magpie Dodge*, will be available in Spring 2000.

Ontario Is The Demon

Her hand on the birch was nothing, then,
Nor her tangled ankles. Her knees did not tremble,
What a relief, she was virtuous among lakes.
Our TV show about cold and dirty lake people

Was flooded in cold bright water. So I saw
Her hard bright nipples, she insisted I brush
Them with my hand's cracked back. As though
I hadn't knelt in crushed pine needles! Me my own self

Talking like a loon between her strong springy legs,
Shunting her strong knee over my neck, to the West.

Hypothetically

Say that lately you've been a bit of an ogre. The weather
Has sucked, everyone keeps squawking at you, your health
Is a bit screwed up, nothing's pretty enough to put your eye
On. Assume that you go hang

About around mountains, become another mouth in a bar
At the base of the hill. Hockey and work to fall back on,
Though. Say pretty soon you've dyed-blond hair and requisite
Tattoos, and you fall in love and pretty soon, two daughters.

Eight years later, a helicopter pops up over the mountain,
And you're just getting over a vicious cold. Weeks of anger
Unaccountably follow, you're so sick of mountains. Daughter
Number one, birthmarked, says "Lately you've been a bit of an ogre."

Letter to the Skyscrapers

You dwarf nothing, I feel a shabby grin-faced
Exuberance among your grey flanks

Anyway, and in the mountains I miss you.
Can't you leave me alone, with your weight

And vulnerability? Towers, I'm slave to your
Windowed constellations: the Party,

The Television Family, the Lonely
One. I love your star charts of backlit lives,

But you don't love me back, my built creatures,
Buttressed, wired, piped, designed, maintained

Creatures. You'll live forever, unless a tremor
Knocks you down. Keep scraping the sky, I ask you.

Harold Rhenisch

Harold Rhenisch (1958-) was born and raised on an orchard in BC's Similkameen Valley. In 1992, he moved to 108 Mile Ranch on BC's Caribou Plateau, the high country between the Fraser and Thompson rivers. He is the author of eight books of poetry, most recently, *Taking the Breath Away*, 1998, and *Fusion*, 1999.

The Summer Philosophers

The philosophers
take blankets
to the water
and lie on grass

Where once were lungs,
beehives throb
Bees flit down
the meadows of their veins

a hawk hunts
in the high sky
of their fingers
A chalk wind blows

Of this life they are unaware
They watch each raindrop
fall and see within them
the world entering their words

world upon world
sparkling green and blue
If you ask
how does the rain taste

the philosophers
will look up
from black volumes
and say it does not at all

Like the sound
of a door
returning to the frame
the cry of birth

returning to its throat
the crash of a wave
returning to its beach
the hand returning

to the mind Now the rain
has stopped
The philosophers
drink the heat

Their words return
heavy with pollen
and the greatest

of emptinesses
wells over them
in cool waves

The World in a Blade of Grass

Whole countries to move into.
First scat of bear on high passes. 6:00 am.

                              Whole valley a salmon
diving into earth.

Gravel scattering.

                    Grey light of water passing through rain.

What is water? What earth?
                              As the river talks: rain.

— Fish condensing out of current
and taking a fly.

— Lip trembling at a kiss, eager bodies
vanishing into a moment,

        the world stretching out from horizon to horizon,
            small as a thumbnail, movement,

        a bead of dew condensed from a black birch twig
        in moon. Light.

                    That. Dante's valley.
        Dante's night.
        Soft.   That.

Shane Rhodes

Shane Rhodes (1973-) has published poetry in magazines across Canada and has been an editor with *The Fiddlehead, filling Station* and *Qwerty*. His first book of poetry is *The Wireless Room*. He lives in Calgary, Alberta.

Whippoorwill

(caprimulgus vociferus)

This is memory's memory of forgetting
a thought that exists only as sound at the
edge of a sky a noise you turn to
expecting nothing for it's made of
nothing but your turning and a sound
more silent than a black and white
and these are the thoughts
making the sun go down as the
last visible itch is gathered
between their wings, goat suckers,
mosquito eaters, whales of the sky,
endings start in their call—more
night than morning, more sunset
than day—they show us to our seats
put the film in backwards
and leave us in the trailer.

As Dust Breaks Over Us

Lilacs unbloomed, like a kind of promise
through the middle of winter, a time,
however merciful, vengeful or indifferent,
chiselled into the snow-bound paths
of our warm-wanting. And I remember
this time of year the look in my father's face
whenever he killed something. It was
a step beyond love, so sure and deep.
To have adopted the wreckage, married it,
as a part of style, the turning mobile formed
and deformed by that which would erase it
from the air I breathe. The apartment walls,
their dramaturgy sizzling into the dream which is,
right now, this instant, tearing us in two.
The air so charged with paths, any moment
would not be the wrong one. Of our midland—
scarves flickering behind our necks—tour,
admittedly much has been forgotten
and we will need much recalling
if we are to get out of this season: blue plum,
saskatoon, high-bush cranberry, chokecherry, wild grapes.
Their names wound the tongue. We hardly remember
how or where the heat fits together with this flesh.
Was it June or July or vice versa?
And in my mind, the pornographic stir of waves.
Flocks of yellow birds displace the sky
with straw colour wings rising from oil soaked reeds.
We would sit there, on the edge of his bidding,
his hair like gilded air. The sky captured
in the distant water, where it plays along the crests
of waves, fenced and tamed. And we forget
the natural pain that makes us. How I think I
only knew my father when he was hurting,
or being hurt. I picture him in the doorway,
the light from the hall streaming around him,

his arms raised to the air in violation
or fear, it was hard to tell which.
The gap between promise and pronouncement—
where the fishes swim. But the night will not
stop for the hotdog stands, and the local rowdy bars,
passing like a rolling pin over leavened dough
where our prayers are fixed between mouth
and suspected ear. But no, not that,
not in the least, haven't you been listening either?
The season has precluded it, abandoned to excess,
nothing more, and we have chased it down.
From the poem, a woman reaches toward us
from her dishevelled bed, her skin wrapped
in meridians, tropics, climata. She reaches
but her arms are warped by the optics of that place
or by the tears brimming in her eyes or ours, and we
cannot tell if she, like a pendulum in mid-swing, is
attracted or repelled, coming or going. I can
only do so much. We can only do so much.
Perhaps her mother is mad or her lover calling?
She waits for us but will not speak. Apogee. Another layer
to which we thought, ages ago, the last. Pisces.
Aries. There are moments where we edge toward
dissolution and nothing we know will drag us back.
No, snow ice-glazed. No, the ice itself like porcelain
freshly baked. The gods, "tossing them off like underwear,"
promise nothing. But perhaps a memory from a distance,
curving the present back into the past and so
our orbits go undiminished. Days pile up at the door.
You remember for no reason your father's face.
The light, when it comes, will arrive, will
falter, will drop to our feet in a motion
it has neither wanted nor longed for.

Jay Ruzesky (1965-) was born in Edmonton, Alberta, but was raised in Saskatoon, Winnipeg, Thunder Bay, Calgary, and Kelowna. He now lives in Victoria, BC, where he teaches at Malaspina University-College. His poems, stories, essays and art criticism have appeared in numerous publications across Canada, and his most recent book, *Writing on the Wall*, was published in 1996.

Jay Ruzesky

Blue Himalayan Poppies

The stems, in their happiness, wave goodbye,
a dart-pattern of spear grass caught
against the black dog's ankle.
Seeds and their smallness, the way they
ride toward the future always.
Such hope makes unlikely light
from the most distant stars possible.
Later in the day they'll drop
into the warm earth.
I never guessed you
would have crossed some great distance
to settle
everywhere in my arms.

*

How was I to know
this, briefly, like the touch
of smallest fingers, after
a long winter and the
Chinese New Year. End
of the year of the dog,
beginning of the year
of the pig. Does it matter?
Maybe not, except summer now,
full of you and how the sun

catches in spray,
rocks below and the edge moving
further away.

*

This morning
I read the poems my friend sent:
postmarks from Izmir and Parma.
Sometimes I think this house,
the mortgage—my god there's a
station wagon in the driveway—
even you, sometimes I think, even you.
I am jealous of languages I don't understand,
mosques with roofs like round fruit.
The seeds of fruit that can't grow
unless a bird digests them,
sprouted like second spines.
The planet revolves under our feet,
around the sun, around
the centre of the centre,
as in the living room
I hold you tight and spin
to the sound of Billie Holiday.

*

Most seeds are lifted by wind.
This afternoon I blew
white dandelions across the yard.
There are days meant for us
when the light is trying to tell us something.
Even the blue Himalayan poppy,
which blooms once perfectly before dying,
is showing off.
I talk in your mouth
and you open bird-like
to swallow words.
This is my pleasure.
You like the round ones best:

igloo, overalls, loop, moon, shoe.
There is nothing in this milky world
as small as your breath.

*

Did you know the coconut
is the only seed that migrates
by water to new islands?
They collapse on the beach after
all that time of waves
passing them hand to hand,
To live in a place like this you must first
imagine it.
Already I am sad for anything
you missed while you were here.
But I walk with you until you sleep.
Somewhere is
the palm at the end of the mind
and high in its branches a bird,
red feathers declaring
I am here.

Sue Sinclair

Sue Sinclair (1972-) grew up in St. John's, Newfoundland, and now lives in Toronto. She has published fiction, poetry, and reviews in journals across Canada; her first book of poetry, *Open Doors*, will be published in 2001.

Red Pepper

Forming in globular
convolutions, as though growth
were a disease. A patient
evolution toward even greater
deformity. It emerges
from under the leaves thick
and warped as melted plastic,
its whole body apologetic:
the sun is hot.

Put your hand on it. The size
of your heart. Which may look
like this, abashed perhaps,
growing in ways you never
predicted.

It is almost painful
to touch, but you can't help
yourself. It's so familiar.
The dents. The twisted symmetry.
You can see how hard it has tried.

Green Pepper

Glossy as a photograph, the bent
circumference catching
the light on its rim. Like a car's
dented fender, the owner desperate
to assess the damage, unable
to say, like the sun, *it can't
be helped.*

Conspicuous and irregular
all its life, it was born
with its eyes shut tight,
as though there really were a collision
it was trying to avoid. But it hasn't
happened yet—there is only
the impact of light: it has never

been in love, never drifted apart,
never fantasized about another
fragrant vegetable, never
been flattered, never been denied,
never wanted more than it has.
Its life is governed
by absence:

the gleam of white
on its hollow body.

March

The car ticks like a cricket,
its engine cooling. Left
to itself it tries to forget
speed, come to grips with where
it wishes it came from: the green
middle of nowhere. At times
like this, a spring thaw,
all of us marooned on curbs
start to think this way.

It pretends not to see itself
in puddles. Ignores chrome
and polish and thinks of a place
far away, a place so small
you could hold it in your palm, so complete
it could only have been imagined.
Ask your mother: there was never
a Sunday drive, no aunt or uncle
in the country. But what are you to do
when even the car remembers the green
sides of the road, the bright air,
how its pistons snapped?
It is entirely convinced: as the heat
dissipates it feels its body
shrink and almost believes
it's going back.

Ricardo Sternberg

Ricardo Sternberg (1948-) was born in Rio de Janeiro and currently lives in Toronto, Ontario, where he is a professor of Brazilian and Portuguese literature at the University of Toronto. He has published two books, *The Invention of Honey*, 1990, and *Map of Dreams*, 1996, and his work has appeared in a number of Canadian and American magazines.

Map of Dreams

* * *

I, Diogo, son of Juan
and Catarina Queluz,
terrified, true enough,
by the sea that roils

and hisses round our ship,
but being otherwise
of sound mind, bequeath
what little is mine:

its dark sun ringed
in mother-of-pearl,
to my sister, Angela,
my rosewood guitar:

To my brother, Luis,
my horse, saddle and spurs;
(the boots do not fit him
and go to my cousin Ramon).

My hunting gun, my dogs,
given me by my father
who also died at sea,
I leave to my brother Carlos;

The Catalogue of Grief,
The Romance of Seven Sages
and The Labyrinth of Fortune
I leave to my sister Isvera

but Claudia Particella
l'amante del Cardinale
is an evil book and so
I leave it to the bonfire

and ask destroyed, unread,
the five volumes of my diary
buried beneath the third
floorboard of my room.

To the pharmacist I leave
my stuffed Antarctic penguin,
my collection of fossils
and The Healing Herbs.

Green as her eyes are green,
green as sometimes the sea,
I give back to Marina
the sweater she knit me.

Let her each day undo
one knot until the whole
is undone: Let her then
turn away and forget me.

Jonah

He, who would not show
his face to Moses,
who drove poor Job
to the brink of despair
comes to pester me now
disguised in the shape
of this minute insect.

No doubt he is making
inordinate demands:
that I build him an ark
or slay my first born
or move to the suburbs
where, covered in ash,
I impress upon the deaf
the magnificence of the word.

Who can decipher this buzz,
save that it signals his anger.
I know enough to stay awake:
dreams return me to the boat
that rocks, unsteady,
until that sailor is cast
into the maw of a giant fish.

Tomorrow, forthwith, to Nineveh.

selena tandon

selena tandon (1976-) was born and raised in Toronto. Her poems have appeared in Canadian journals and magazines, and *Shaktee Kee Awaz*, an anthology of South Asian and Indo-Caribbean women's writing.

in mumbai
(for deepa mehta)

1
the tears have not
stopped running in mumbai tonite
brown streams of
screams etch rivers
into roads
winding
like women
around bodies of
women
around cities and countryside
where women with
women
seek dry corners
of saris
pulled to comfort those
women
who sit in
puddles of grief
& desire

2
bolo beti
    that is all i can say
    what i cant say is
kush ney muthleb hai
    what i can't say is
    the language between us
    the breath that strains when you ask
beti appkhi shadi kab hoghi
    this distance between words that i form
    stretches far beyond words that i understand
    & you are content to hear me reply
hoon ney

3
the cinemas are packed full
with men
grabbing their crotches
while shiva sets fire to
projector screens

4
asay dheko
    like this
ankhe bund karke
hoon dus
hoon key dheko
    outturned bellies
    brown skin
    the richness of earth
ma ajo
asay dheko

5
shiva has not moved since
we arrived here
not for a moment has he shifted his gaze
from our hands
clutching desperation
youve drawn blood
cleaned with the
edge of my sari
already red raw
silk

6
the censors let it pass
& i screamed
ma heard me
ran to my room
held me   ran
to my room
already filled with the screams
of dry throats
hoarse from screaming

7
in mumbai
i sleep with a goddess
under my arm
to show ma
i will say
i found her lying beside me
her sari soaked wet around her ankles

John Terpstra

John Terpstra (1953-) was born in Brockville, Ontario, and currently lives in Hamilton, where he is a self-employed cabinet maker and woodworker. He has published six books of poetry, his most recent being, *The Church Not Made with Hands*, 1997, and *Devil's Punch Bowl*, 1998.

To God, as a Small Pest

The squirrel scrambling, light-as-air, over the roof
is you, is it not? The roaming slope
to peak, across and down, scritches
delicate as destruction,
                              shows that old animal
spirit trying to find a way in, never yet
poking a grey head past the edge of the skylight,
so I may see.

                        I believe, now,
you have no pride; an imagination
that ranges wildly, seizing any
shape that fits, adopting
what'll do,
                   with a relentless playfulness,
and your insidious intent;
                              and I resist
this recognition, as strongly
as the gnawing at my fascia, soffit,
that I imagine comes next, and tense and listen for.

I rather looked for you in the birds gathered
about the feeder, the many separate
thoughts one has, the argue and agreement
of wings, and a hungry abandon to the truth
of contending against another winter's advent.

New this Fall is the balled nest of leaves no bird
comes near, that the highest-reaching branches of the ash
lift eye-level to the attic room I hole in.
You're home. Comfort and warning
co-habit,

      as when I stood below, preparing
breakfast, and happened to look, you
halfway up the trunk, our eyes locked
and I wondered what,
        what was that small round
black thing
you held in your mouth?

James Joyce and the Equator

When James Joyce encompassed all the known
world in his book *Finnegans Wake*, his initial
impulse was to publish the entire effort on a tape
wound round a reel much like the reels
we now have in recording studios
and at home
In this way he anticipated the great
aural breakthrough of the fifties

He envisioned a single edition of the huge
work, printed on a roll of canvas
the size of a ferris wheel, and mounted
on an equatorial island

his one long sentence unwinding
word by word in slow revolution
like the earth, stretching out
across the continents and oceans
that had not always been there
but would
now

        This was the great long railway, laid
and laying the great Atlantic cable
in one, but all the way around
He saw himself, with some ceremony
seamlessly stitching beginning to end
in a kind of reverse ribbon-cutting
having proved the technology existed
within
        But by the time the author's finished draft
was complete, it ran some six hundred pages
had taken considerably longer
than anyone cared to reminisce, and also
caused blindness
He was led to perceive his work less
tangibly as paper, pen
and that is why we have what we have
now, and it's just a book
you hardly see anymore

the fine interminate line
his spiralled margination

Priscila Uppal

Priscila Uppal (1974-) is a poet and fiction writer born in Ottawa, Ontario. She lives in Toronto and has published two poetry collections, *How to Draw Blood From a Stone*, 1998, and, *Confessions of a Fertility Expert*, 1999. She is currently working on a third collection of poetry and a book of short stories.

Bone-marrow

Trees know each other by their bark.
Everything alive has developed a language.
Even thunder, even death.

Children are obsessed with mirrors
trying to pry the glass free
to release the twin who understands their every move
and face.

Lovers despair the moment
they no longer find a reflection
in each other's tears.

Look at science:
Desperately in love with itself searching
for solar systems identical to ours.
Signs of life.

For want of bone-marrow
the entire kingdom was lost.

Think about why religions fail.

How to Draw Blood From a Stone

On family afternoons
the digging begins.
It begins with your hands.

You carry the stones like stillborn babies,
lay them down.
So closely the heads rise
from brown wet beds.

You add others when it rains,
when you're sad.
You name them all
by holding them down.

In winter they sit patiently
amongst the cold.
You stare wondering
what they want,
so close to the earth
and still.

This is not a place you go to speak.
The stones bleed through
the soil.

This is not a graveyard.
You can't apologize.

Pretending to Die

When I dug myself into the muddy sand
the waves seemed to roll
with new vigour. The sun burnt delirious
eyelids, I desperately tried, but couldn't
keep closed.

Perchance there would be screams
and sirens, a frantic mob shedding tears
a new mother to cradle my limp
flesh and strap her lips
firmly on mine.

Instead the tide washed in
bearing seaweed and popsicle sticks
a little girl stole my pail
even the sand abandoned me
while the one I loved for three full summers
stepped squarely upon my ribs
and kept on going.

Steve Venright (1961-) was born in Sarnia, Ontario, and lives in Toronto. He is a poet, visual artist and sound composer who has published four books of poetry including, *Straunge Wunder*, 1996, and *Spiral Agitator*, 2000. He is currently at work on a sound sculpture based on the works of Christopher Dewdney.

Steve Venright

Occurrence of Delusional Fixation Involving Winchester Cathedral in Sexually Frustrated Adult Male

He's scolding a cathedral. He blames the cathedral for his depressive state, which he insists could have been averted by the intervention of that edifice. A woman with whom he'd been emotionally involved has left town. Had the cathedral merely started "ringing its bell", he reasons, the woman would not have departed; hence, the possibility of a reconciliation—or perhaps some form of ego-gratifying harassment— would still exist. Logically, he admits that the cathedral could not have been cognizant of the extent to which he "needed that gal". Nevertheless, he reprimands it for simply standing and watching as the object of his desire walked past on her way out of the city. "You could have done *some*thing!" wails the abandoned lover. Justified or not, such derision elicits a peculiar empathy: one cannot help but feel sorry for the old cathedral, its mute architecture bearing the brunt of broken-hearted humanity's deranged plight.

Smargana Lareves

1. This sentence uses only recycled words.
2. Using this sentence for any purpose other than communication or information storage may be dangerous.
3. This sentence began life as an artefact.
4. This sentence has a fixed meaning that does not change, whether spoken in a catacomb or spoken in a conference room.
5. This sentence may be used repeatedly without deterioration, though overuse may lead to apparent diminishment of its significance (and in extreme cases insanity or the delusion of enlightenment).
6. This sentence may be spoken with the impunity of ignorance by animals, or computers, capable of mimicking human speech.
7. This sentence is not immune to polyglot shift: if it has been written, spoken, or otherwise processed in any language other than English, a translation has occurred; in this event, please contact the manufacturer should you wish to be issued the original English language version.
8. This sentence should not be taken literally by pregnant women, or laterally by dyslexics.
9. This sentence may be used to rouse someone from a deep slumber if spoken loudly enough—optimal volume will vary according to proximity of speaker to subject (and density of the sleepstate).
10. This sentence is communicable and may be transmitted orally, or by braille, through photic projection and similar forms of reproduction, via the print medium, telepathically, or by means not yet imagined.
11. This sentence can be stared at without comprehension.
12. This sentence is several anagrams.

Malpractice

Three aspirins and an enema to cure a woman in the throes of labour.
Electroshock therapy to treat a young girl suffering from tonsillitis.
Removal of the gallbladder to heal an elderly male frostbite victim.
A plaster cast over the left forearm and wrist to restore the memory
of a middle-aged female amnesiac.
Circumcision to alleviate the symptoms of a persistent headcold
afflicting a teenage boy.

Linda Waybrant

Linda Waybrant (1957-) is a native Torontonian. She has been published in numerous literary journals and her work took first prize in *Prairie Fire's* long poem contest, 1995. Her first book of poetry, *The Colour of Flight*, was published in 1996. She is a member of the League of Canadian Poets and the watershedBooks co-operative.

it is easy to slip under
a lake perhaps the ocean

& this is an ocean

a lesson in gravity
in confluence

note the angle of waves

the small sky
                between the waves

the open grates
between the waves

the colour of flight

& when she tells her story
she says   fish in small bowls
          gold fish   wrapped wrapped in soft tissue
          one eye left to see free

see the unimaginable—
a child fitting inside easily she climbed into
          the white
          the dumb white
                    of trust
          a child's story: always a door out
          to the empty space of understanding

a conversation on a drive home
one person speaking to another
a horizon with no beginning
no end

we ate donuts in the car while my niece cried

because it was so late
because we liked the cowboy song on the radio
because it was cold outside
how cold do you think it will get?

without light
without heat

because when she tried to spread herself out

she hit her head

landscape   too often defined by what it lacks

a story—
of a small dark place
where a child tries to keep something warm

**my hands have gotten larger lately
also they're stronger
a see thru quality is especially noticeable
when they're beside yours**

(for Frank)

last night I had this dream in a green suit
iridescent suit
very large
later I give the jacket part to you
as a present
I feel kind of unsure about this gift
having worn it one time already
& it being on the rather huge side
but—you say my name
tell much about how you like it
give the cloth a shake
& climb in

as a rule
I size up everything pretty careful—
count words too
but this jacket needs explaining:
it fits like a kid glove
& I can't see no alteration in dimension either way
alarm
sounds like I'm awake

today from memory
I wear my clothes big
I think: expanse of shimmering green

Matt
Yeldon

Matt Yeldon (1973-) was born and raised in
Toronto, Ontario. He is a poet, fiction
writer and occasional stage actor whose
work has appeared in Canadian journals
and magazines. He is currently completing
an undergraduate degree at York University.

Dunmore Throop

still readable   despite snow
slamming the middle
of Pennsylvania roadsigns
into patterns of gunshot

unless you were the deer
failing to evade human eyes
on a side-road far from your
home named after a sound
in your sleek white throat

frightening in our ears
like a flush of water off the drum
or an attempt to say
I'm lost   I give up
hand me over to the animals

"rlur" : the history of a sound

...

derived from the Japanese, an interjection
suggesting one's inner-child's sheer contentment
in the face of apathy.

...

(instead of privacy)

he offers her the illusion of privacy,
the permanence of an inconstant home—
shifting paper doors;
the painted histories of war
and poetry on unrolled silk;
the tapestries from former lovers;
and bamboo floors,
slippery and resistant to resonance

(to preserve her dulcet sounds).

...

she whirs it out a bird's way, into the narrowest island's wind,
to where the coughings of crows go—resolved to be caught
solely by the tuned ears of fishermen.

...

when he is sleepwalking,
able to blacken his unsandled feet over a day's worth of dust,
weaving in and out of the latest renovation—
the thin mutable labyrinth only a man would use
to curb a woman's love—
he reframes the streets of Tokyo in his dreams
so that birds are thrown off.

....

because innocence, she imagines
is not something one is easily reaccustomed to.

...

sometimes her throat, still coral-coloured
by light of a single lantern by the bed,
grows fervent with the need to deliver.

...

she wonders if his gift itself is redundant,
and not the way the gift is bestowed:
a kimono—all shimmer like the centre of a peacock's plume;
a bright-coloured sash to fasten around the midsection;
tailored so that a woman's neck is left susceptible
to the faintest of breath—shares intention
with a complex system of packaging.

...

a plan to smuggle it home:
she will tuck the sound between her two favourite teeth
or under tongue to keep the lemondrops company.

(once safe, when the passengers snore and crane
their necks because the altitude has tempted them
to keep on rising, she will press her little nose to a window,
resent a fleet of machines in the sky,
irresponsive to the confidence of birds).

...

what the silhouette uttered through the thin white paper
a full month before leaving, leaving
fingers unsettled—
in the room where he watched—
on a tea cup
resting on a cushion
the size of a lung.